AF429011

Hex codes, or hexadecimal codes, are a way to represent colors in digital devices and web design. Each hex code refers to a very specific color. A hex color is expressed as a six-digit combination of numbers and letters, preceded by a pound sign or hashtag, defined by its mix of red, green, and blue (RGB). The first two letters or numbers refer to red, the next two refer to green, and the last two refer to blue.

The color values are defined as values between 00 and FF. Hex codes are a universal way to describe colors. This book is specifically about fruit colors.

A is for açaí berry

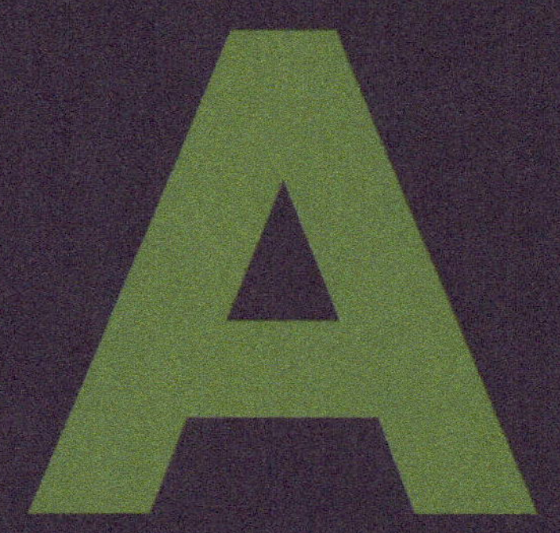

#42314B

a is for avocado

a

#568203

B is for banana peel

B

#FFE774

b is for blueberry

b

#464196

C is for coconut

#965A3E

c is for cranberry

c

#9E003A

D is for desert lime

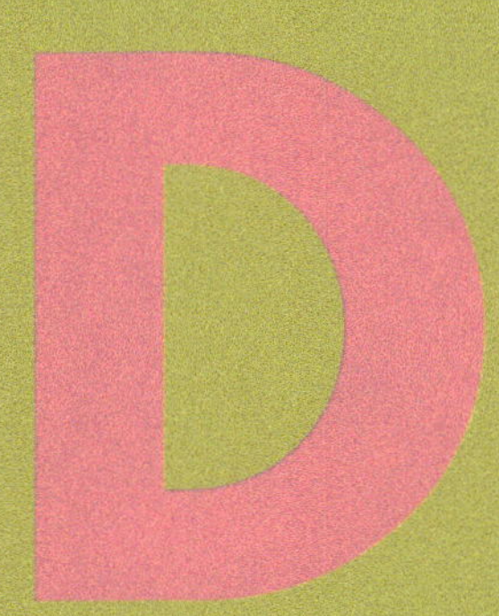

#C2B639

d is for dragon fruit

#F35D8B

E is for eggplant

E

#311465

e is for elderberry

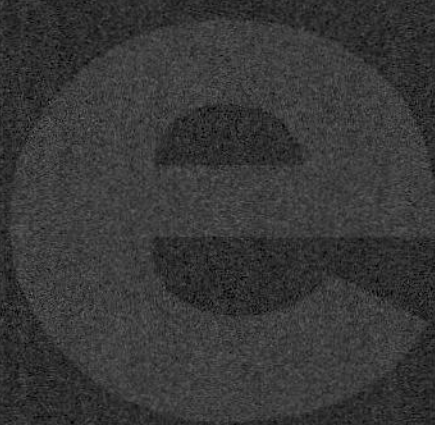

#2E2249

F is for feijoa

F

#A3D991

f is for fig

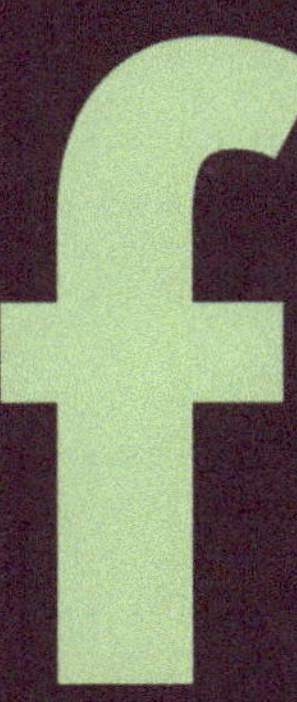

#532D3B

G is for goji berry

G

#B91228

g is for grapefruit juice

g

#EE6D8A

H is for honeydew

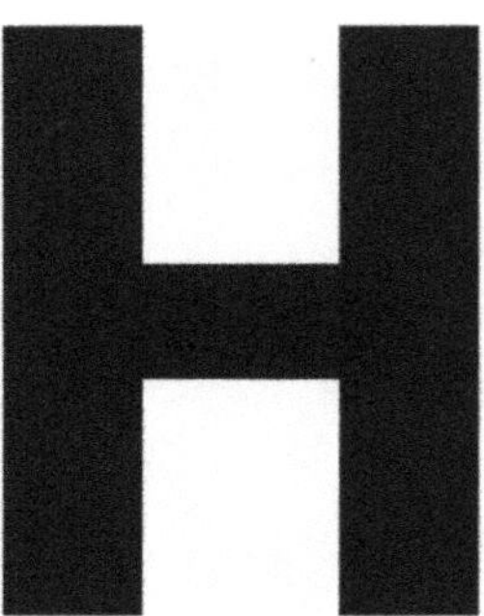

#F0FFF0

h is for huckleberry

h

#5B4349

I is for icaco

I

#D8C3C9

i is for italian plum

#51354A

J is for jackfruit

#F7C680

j is for juniper berry

#D7C3CF

K is for kiwi

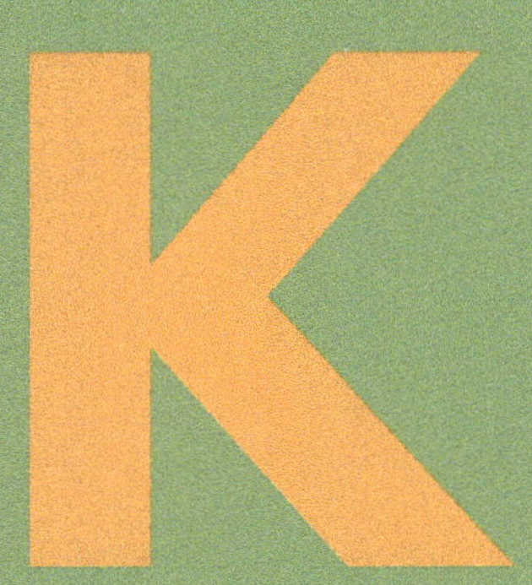

#7AAB55

k is for kumquat

k

#FB9912

L is for lemon

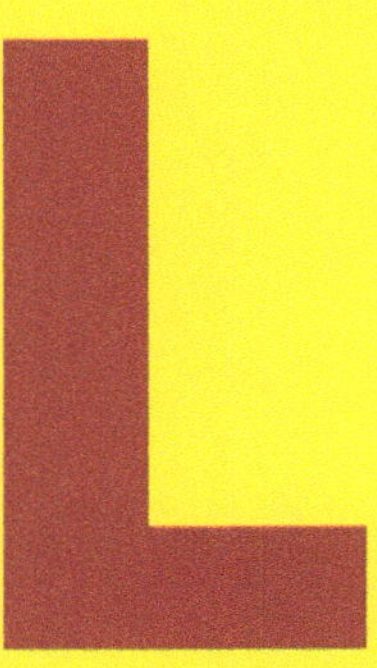

#FFF700

l is for lychee

l

M is for mango

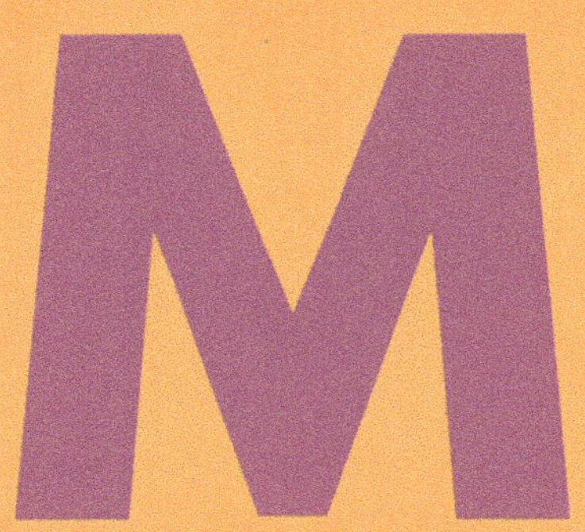

#FFA62B

m is for mulberry yogurt

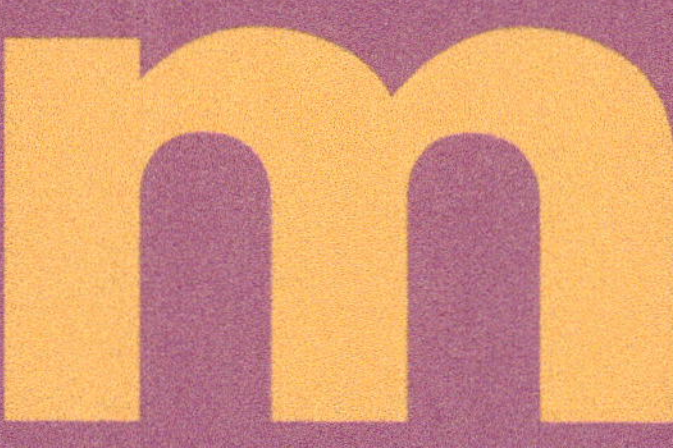

#C54B8C

N is for nectarine

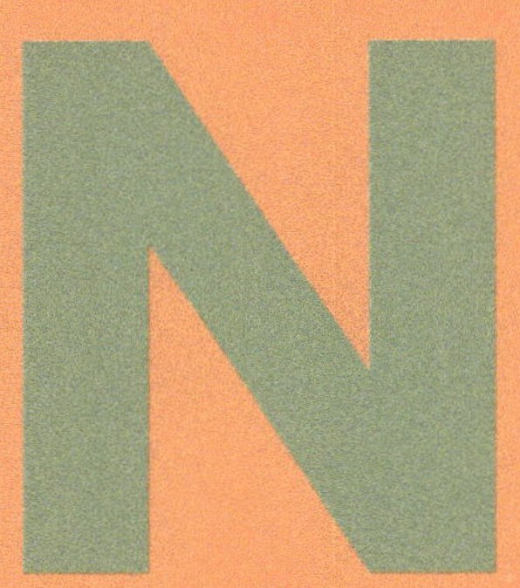

#FF8856

n is for nopal

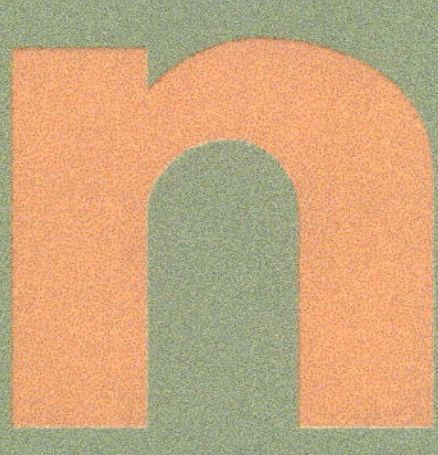

#8EAA77

O is for olive

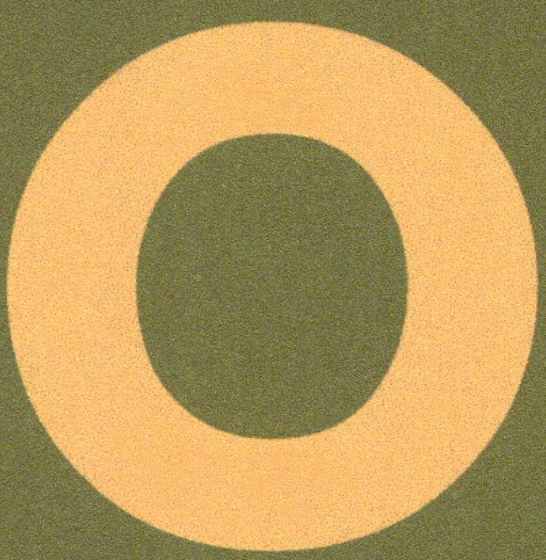

#7F7D07

o is for orange

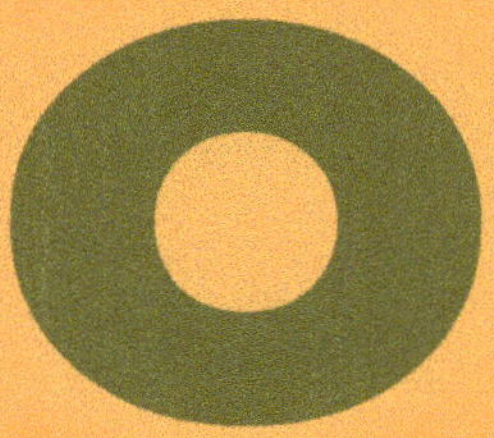

#FFA500

P is for pineapple

P

#FFF44

p is for pear

p

#D1E231

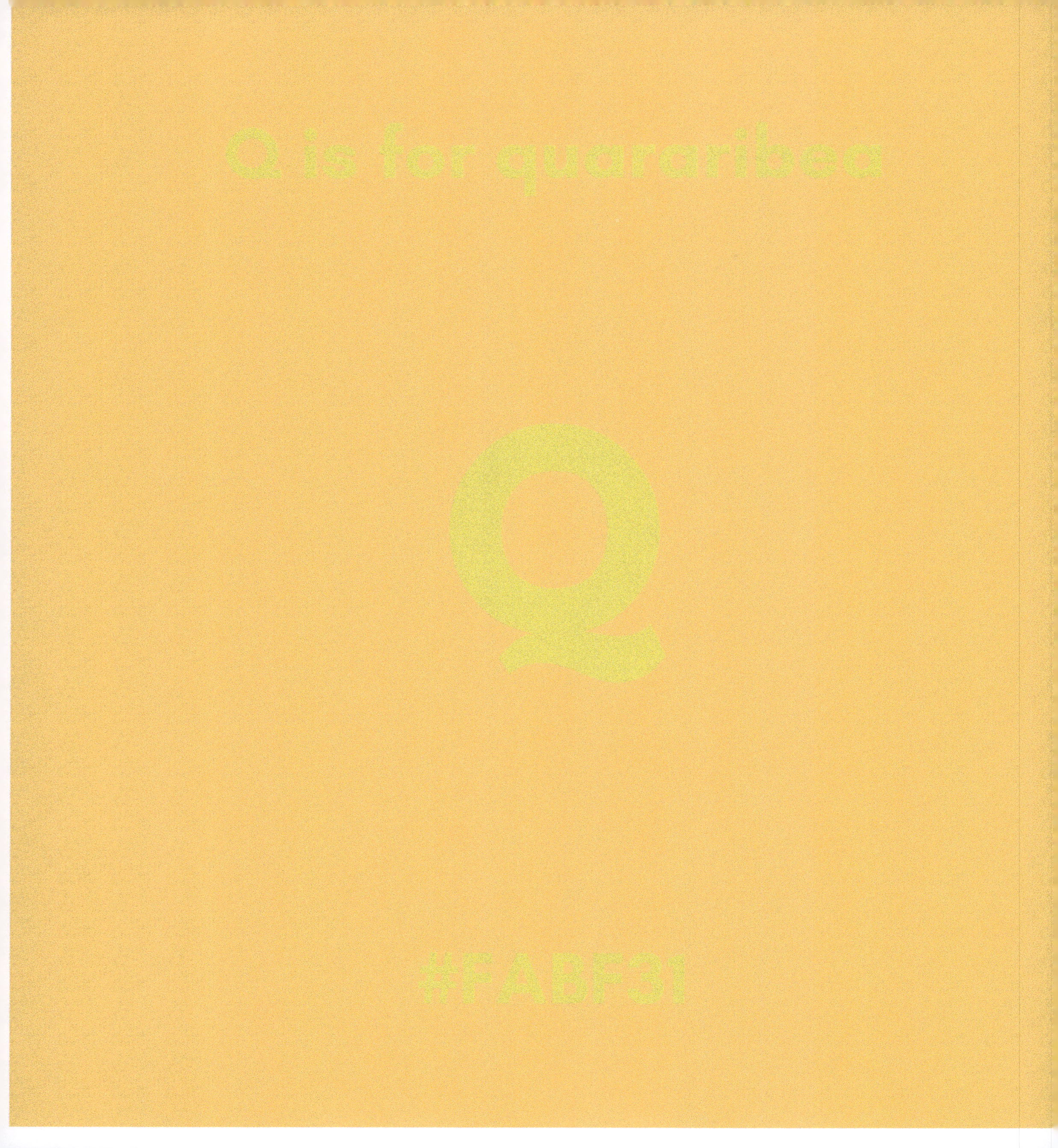

Q is for quararibea
Q
#FABF31

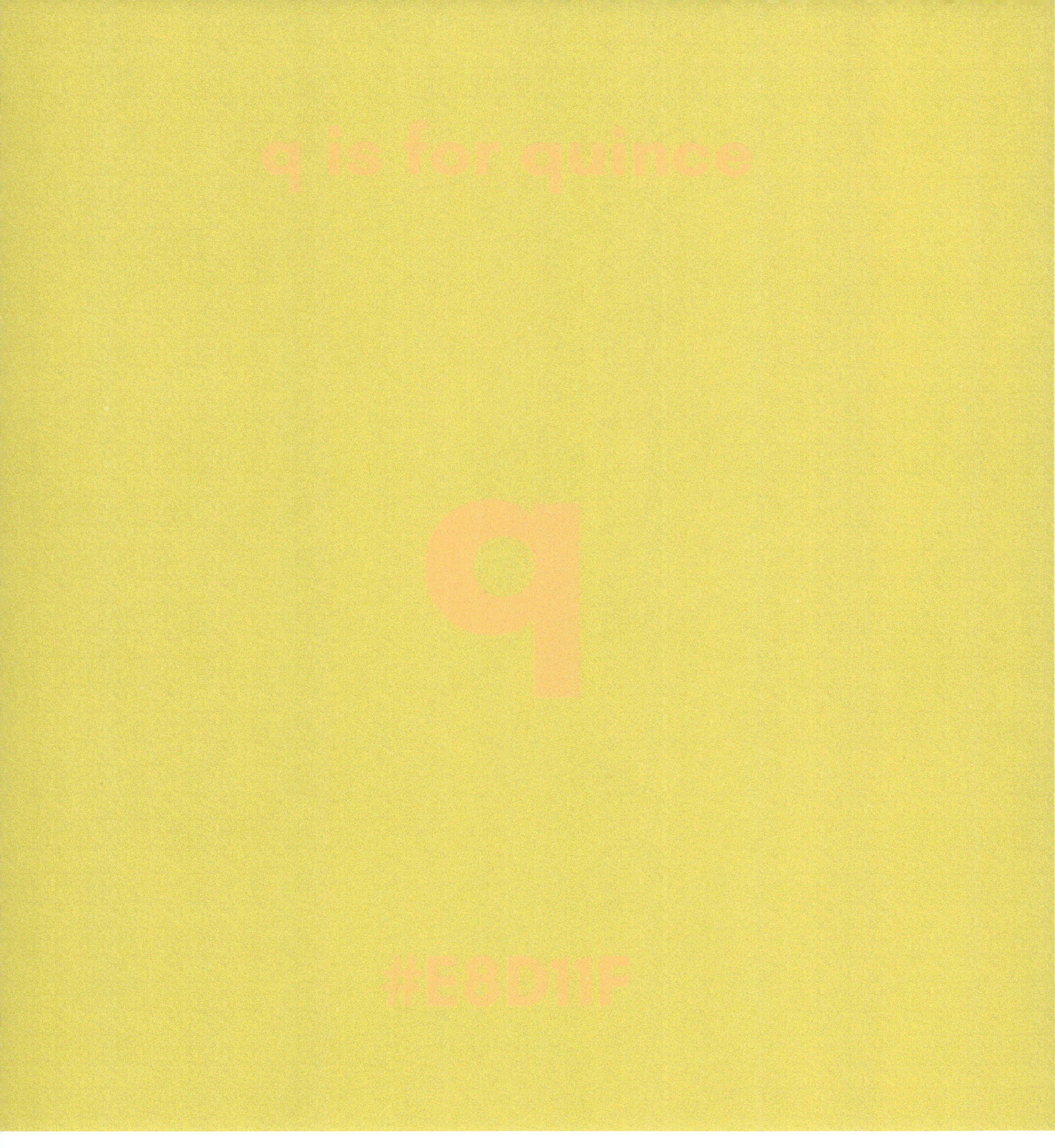
q is for quince
q
#E8D11F

R is for raspberry

R

#B00149

r is for rhubarb

r

#77202F

S is for sour cherry

#E04C32

s is for strawberry
s
#FB2943

T is for teaberry

#DC3855

t is for tomato

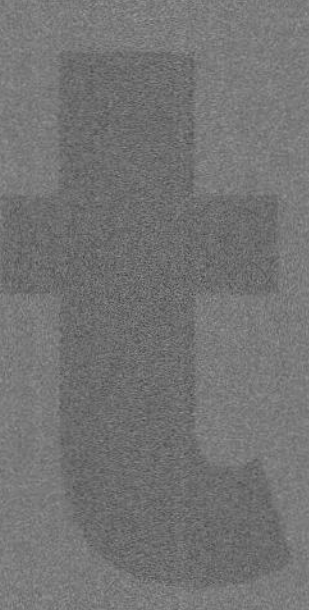

#EF4026

U is for ube

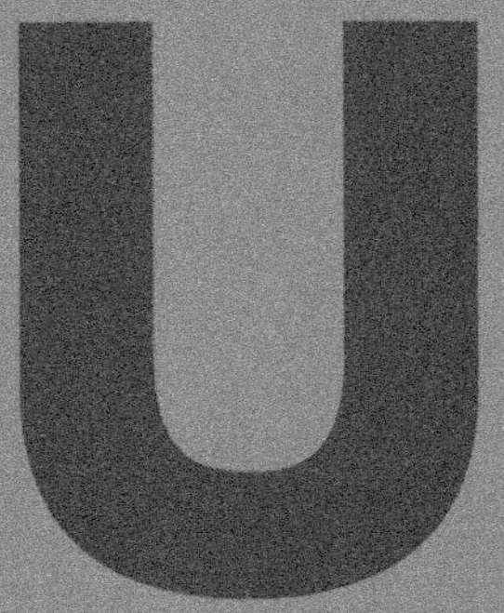

#8878C3

u is for ume

u

#8F4155

V is for vernaccia grapes

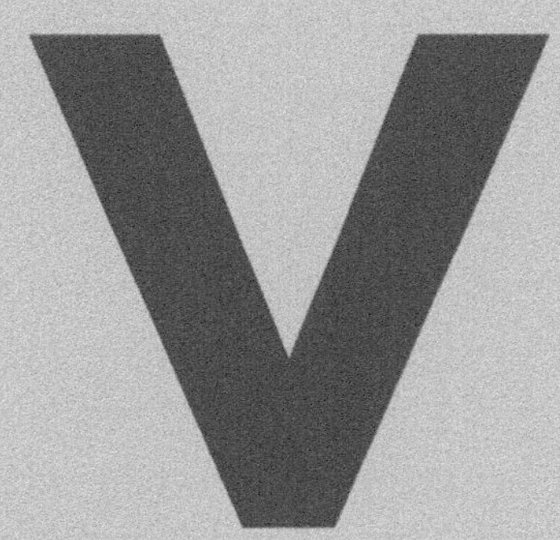

#A6BE47

v is for victoria plum

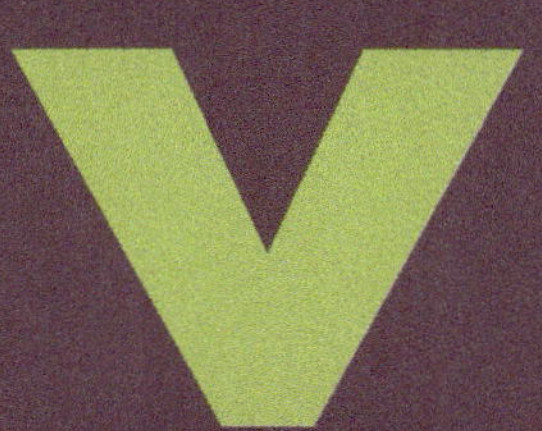

#764A59

W is for watermelon

W

#FD4659

w is for wintermelon

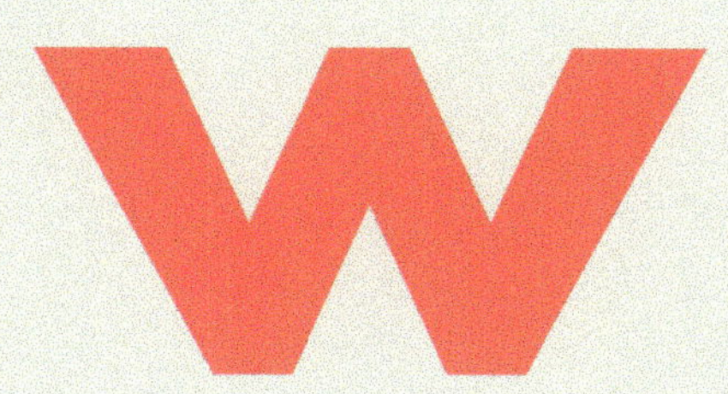

#E3ECD5

X is for xerophyte

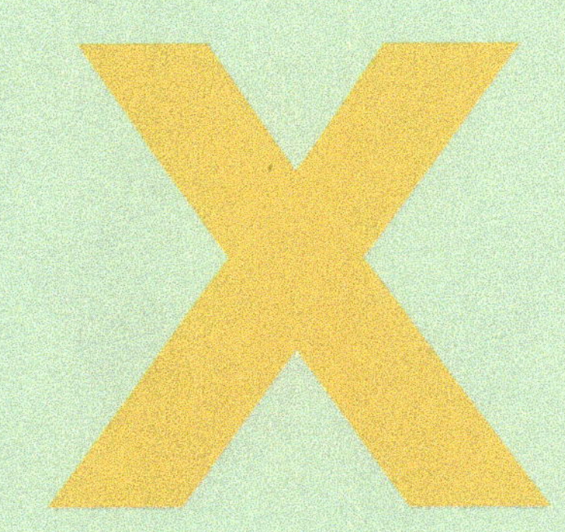

#BFE2BE

x is for ximena

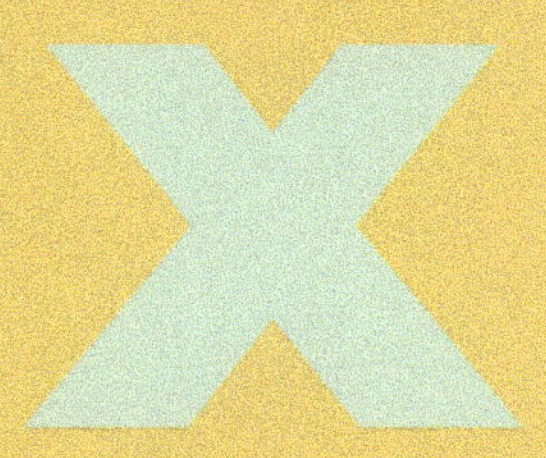

#F2C74A

Y is for yucca

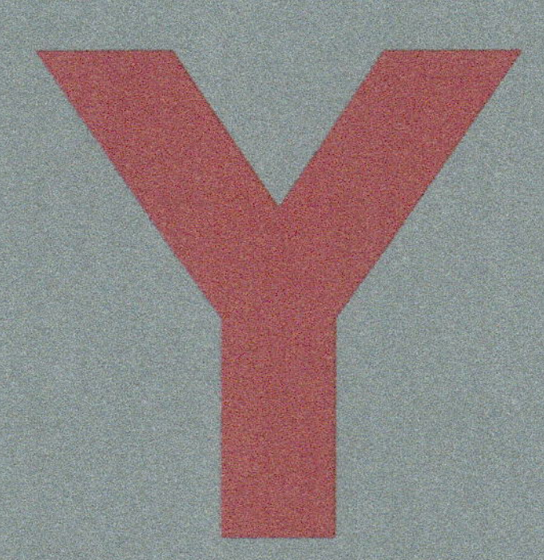

#75978F

y is for yumberry

y

#AA1133

Z is for zarzamora

Z

#713B55

z is for zucchini

Z

#174628

www.ingramcontent.com/pod-product-compliance
Lightning Source LLC
Chambersburg PA
CBHW040153110726
48005CB00018B/2741